T0209096

Survival Wisdom

Motivational Thoughts to Help You Prevail

Rich Hungerford

BALBOA.
PRESS

A DIVISION OF HAY HOUSE

Balboa Press books may be ordered through booksellers or by contacting:

Balboa Press
A Division of Hay House
1663 Liberty Drive
Bloomington, IN 47403
www.balboapress.com.au
1 (877) 407-4847

Print information available on the last page.

ISBN: 978-1-5043-0305-7 (sc)
ISBN: 978-1-5043-0306-4 (e)

Balboa Press rev. date: 06/15/2016

Dedication

To my two greatest heroes; Rebel and Pia, you
are my world I love you with all that I am.
Always stay strong and be fearless! To all my
teachers—past, present, and future—I give sincere
thanks for your selfless gifts of wisdom and for
guiding me onto the path of self-reliance.

Preface

*E*ach year people around the world find themselves in perilous survival situations with the suddenness and total immersion that is characteristic of these situations often serving to catch them off guard and unawares. One minute everything is normal and going as planned, and the next they find themselves caught up in events beyond their control and in many cases fighting for their lives. These situations may manifest in many ways such as being unexpectedly lost in the wilderness, being caught up in the aftermath of a major natural disaster, a severe accident or perhaps something as simple as just being in the wrong place at the wrong time when things go terribly wrong. Life can seem incredibly unfair at times, and the Earth we live on can appear to be uncaring of the many creatures that live upon it. As humans, these major tragedies have the potential to leave us traumatised and devastated. The truth is that bad things simply just happen sometimes and no one is immune from this reality.

Coupled with this understanding is another reality that we are slowly becoming aware of and that is of our increasing collective dislocation from nature. Many of us are blessed with the good fortune to live in first world countries complete with the support of innumerable forms of technology and utilities that go together to make a modern city what it is. It is the collective of all of the little things that make life more prosperous, easier and more comfortable. We consequently witness the ever increasing concentration of people into cities around the globe all seeking the same access to abundance and ease. All of which serves to increase the pressure on natural systems to both make way and provide for burgeoning populations increasingly jammed into focussed geographical spaces.

This circumstance results in fewer and fewer people knowing little if anything about the natural world or their place within it. As each new generation arrives for their turn at life on Earth the relevance of nature decreases even further. In fact, we have become so disassociated with it that we perceive it as unimportant, hostile and largely unnecessary. It is simply something out there, a resource for us humans, that we take from and give little back to. Essentially the natural world and all of the systems that support life in the city remain out of sight and out of mind and life as we know it trundles along in the controlled chaos that frames our day to day existence.

So consequently, when either natural or human-made events destroy and rob from us our precious modernity, few of us possess the knowledge, skill, and experience our forebears once did to function in a world devoid of technology and supply chains. Literally, when the lights go out and fail to come back on again, we find ourselves less able to cope with the dark, i.e., the sudden and dynamic change we face, than our predecessors were perhaps able to. They could just apparently do more with less than we who live in a highly manufactured world can do today. If something breaks in our world we need to get a specialist repairer in to fix it or be able to get exactly the right manufactured part for the broken device we seek to repair, if it can be repaired at all. Usually it is just easier for it to be discarded and replaced, added to a landfill site somewhere that has long replaced a natural wetland or forest. Whereas those who came before us just figured it out and repaired it with tape, wire, intelligence and trial and error. They seemed to be more in touch with both nature and with their hands than we are today. We almost have an attitude of looking down on people who still use their hands to make a living, as though it was some lower form of human existence that we have now transcended. Every parent now wants their child to grow up to be a doctor or a lawyer rather than a carpenter or a farmer. The question then is this, in our quest for ever increasing wealth, prosperity, status, convenience and comfort have we relinquished our capability as humans to be resilient?

Being able to weather the many storms that life throws our way, to cope with significant change, manage risks, make informed choices about what to do next and keep ourselves emotionally balanced throughout the journey of change seems to now be something we increasingly struggle with. The above are the constituent attributes of personal resilience, that ability to cope no matter what and bounce back from any difficulties we face. It is these attributes that appear to be in decline within individuals living modern lifestyles. Essentially, we have forsaken a large portion of our innate and hard learned hominid resilience in favour of comfort and convenience. We have consistently opted to take the easy path and failed to exercise our resilience skills sufficiently. For to do so involves some necessary exposure to pain and discomfort as it is only in that space that we grow and learn to cope.

Survival situations are defined as times when we are seeking to meet only our most basic needs, those concerning protection from the elements, water to drink and food to eat in order to remain alive. Survival as a concept is purely about life support. When confronted with a lack of basic shelter, drinking water, and food or struggling to deal with the perceived hopelessness of total isolation, injury, illness, or death the innermost facets of human resilience are exposed. A lack of control, disruption to our perception of "normal," disorientation, confusion, increases in discomfort, hunger, thirst, fatigue, illness, injury, fear, and more mean that we face significant physiological and psychological challenges to remain alive at these times.

Disasters can occur suddenly, at any time or at any place, and can affect anyone. The greatest mistake we humans regularly make in ensuring our own survival is convincing ourselves that "It can never happen to us." Bad things can and do happen. They happen worldwide with monotonous regularity and to unsuspecting and unprepared people everyday. Identifying and accepting this fact is the first step in truly preparing to survive anything. I compare the attitude of the survivor to that of the warrior. The tenacity, determination, motivation, dedication to training, and willingness to fight hard for what is important so characteristic of a warrior's attitude are all echoed in a survivor's mindset.

This little book of survival wisdom is written with the hope that it will assist you to prepare emotionally for a survival event. Where the mind goes, the body will follow. Preparing and conditioning the mind to weather difficult times is a core aspect of survival training the world over that receives very little attention. For the most part, when we think of preparing for survival, our minds race to what equipment we will need and what physical skills we will need to develop. My considerable first-hand experience has shown me that unless we successfully control our emotions under duress, we lessen our survival prospects significantly, no matter how much equipment and skill we have at our disposal. Our level of emotional intelligence is a critical factor in our survivability. Emotional intelligence is understanding the emotions we experience when things go wrong, and managing them effectively. It is an ability to filter what thoughts we allow ourselves to pay attention to. Further it involves understanding and, more importantly, empathising with the respective individual emotional experiences that those around us are also feeling during a survival situation. All of this is important if we (ourselves) are to avoid the dangers a lack of self-confidence, trust, belief, faith, mettle, conviction, self-reliance and level-headedness may represent to our ongoing existence. We need to be in a position of internal strength and power to prevail and to provide real leadership to our group during periods of hardship. Learning to rapidly accept our situation, control our fears, focus our anger and frustration, and remain strong throughout all we face is the magic bullet of survival. It always has been!

The core message here is that *you* must quickly come to understand that *you* are in control of *you*. *You* often cannot control or significantly influence events and people outside of *you,* so focus on that which you can influence. *You* choose what thoughts to pay attention to, and *you* create your own future. I have read so many stories of people literally giving up when facing survival situations, being defeated not by the situation itself but by their thoughts. I have also observed this pattern of thoughts shaping outcomes during Special Forces selection activities. During these events, physically tough soldiers experience an environment where every ounce of drive and motivation must come from within. The incredibly high failure rate involved in these activities occurs because the great majority give up and voluntarily withdraw from the course of their own volition. Despite the large number of withdrawals, each year a small number get through and go on to become part of the Special Forces community.

What is the "thing" that makes the difference? What is it that few seem to possess and the majority don't? How can we change that proportion of pass/fail so that more people can prevail when the going gets tough? My observation as an instructor is that those who make it through are the ones who are able to dig deep when the body's strength has long since ebbed. At that time, they are powered solely by an absolute force of will, and their ability to tap into that precious resource is what sets them apart from others. They possess the ability to work through immense pain and fatigue and simply keep on keeping on. Observing and experiencing these situations first-hand leaves me in no doubt whatsoever that how you think determines the emotional state you function in, and a poor emotional state leads to failure every time. It is an old cliché, but the enemy is truly within, and only the individual can choose to face that adversary and bring it to heel. When we change our thoughts, we change the outcome. It's that simple, and we can change our thoughts with words.

The use of inspirational anecdotes, affirmations, or words is an incredibly powerful yet simple tool to remind us what is going on within and where we need to refocus our thoughts to prevent ourselves from descending down the slide of negativity and defeatism. This is a common technique in the toolbox of the self-help world. Here we apply it to the most perilous events we may face in life, when the outcome could possibly lead to our demise. What could be more important than equipping ourselves with coping mechanisms to deal with disasters of this magnitude if or when they appear?

The anecdotes and affirmations presented in this book will help you to stay strong and be fearless in the face of calamity. They will assist you to prepare for and handle all that life can throw at you. They are also geared towards making you resilient enough to lead and guide those around you, particularly the ones you love and care for. To lead effectively in the face of a disaster, the leader must first survive! They must consolidate their personal will to survive and their survival mindset. So while survival situations are the focus of this work, you will find the wisdom expressed here is transferable to many aspects of your daily life. This book is ultimately about *preparing* the mind for life when things go wrong, as they so often do. It is about teaching you to accept the situation you face now and, finally, giving you the understanding of how to maintain the mindset of a survivor. If just one soul is preserved in part by the words in this book, the effort of writing it will have been more than worthwhile. Stay strong and be fearless!

A Prayer to the Wisdom of the Universe

Wankan Tanka (Great Spirit), Father Sky, Mother
Earth, old people, forest people ... I give thanks
for your wise counsel, for your love, your guidance
and for your trust in me. May your words be
heard as my words such that the wisdom of the
ancients is not lost and that we living humans
may again find our way back to being good
custodians of the Earth. May we live in peace!

Section 1

Preparing Your Survival Mindset

To survive a life and death situation you must—above all, completely, and without a single doubt—believe that you will prevail, no matter your circumstance! You must have no doubt at all, only absolute, unwavering faith that you will get through this.

To prepare for survival, you must adopt the attitude of a warrior and train your mind, body, and spirit. Only in this way will you understand what it really means to be resilient

Survival ability begins with knowledge, knowledge
builds self-confidence; together, they serve to control
fear. Control of fear creates opportunity for action.
Action equates to self-responsibility.
Self-responsibility fosters self-reliance.
Self-reliance equates to resilience.
The resilient become leaders.
In times of great uncertainty and fear,
people need resilient leaders.

Never confuse gear or equipment with actual survival
capability. You must look inwards to find the tools
that assist you to make it through tough times.
Your survival is always hinged to your attitude,
so choose one that will allow you to prevail.

Prepare well, survive easily.

Discomfort and inconvenience are valuable
experiences that teach us to cope with adversity.
Do not shy away from these great teachers.

You can read, watch, and study survival and
bushcraft skills all you like, but until you convert
that interest to actual "dirt time," it counts
for little. So don't count on just your research
to keep you alive, get out there and do it.

Muscles do not ensure your survival; only your mindset, determination, and tenacity can do that. Be sure to train each of the latter as much as—if not more than—the former.

Your body is the vehicle that you will likely be attempting to survive in. Prepare it before hand, feed it well, train it well and understand how to keep it strong and resilient. The importance of this principle far outweighs going out and buying another survival gadget that you put in your back pack. In many cases you'll be asking your body to carry that back pack at some point, so get the vehicle prepared before you load it up.

The more you learn about your body's physical and psychological requirements before you face adversity, the less you have to learn about these things during an ordeal. You will have enough things on your mind at that time, so do all you can to reduce the burden by preparing beforehand.

"Knowledge weighs nothing,
so carry as much as you can of it
in all things related to the survival of yourself,
your family, and your community."

—Captain Graham Brammer (Ret.)
Australian Army Survival Wing

Good preparation for disasters and crises
is more about how you condition yourself to think
than it is about what you carry in your pack.

If you never consider the what-ifs in life, you will not expect the unexpected. Accordingly, when calamity is upon you, you will be stunned and unable to respond. To *prepare* is intelligent, to *plan* is logical, and to do neither is to accept failure before you even begin the game.

Bad things happen to people just like you all the time, every day, just as they were thinking exactly what you are thinking right now: *that won't happen to me!* So choose to do something about it. Make a choice to be ready.

Plan! Prepare! Practice!
What could I do if A happens,
B occurs, or C manifests?
What do I need to deal with those things?
What alternatives are there likely to be?
What do I need to research, practice,
rehearse, and upskill on?
I choose to plan for survival.
I choose to start that plan now!

"Proper prior planning and preparation
prevents pathetically poor performance."

—Anonymous Australian soldier

Learn to recognise the stars and the
constellations in the night sky, and they will
soon become familiar old friends. No matter
how far from home you find yourself,
look up, and there they are, friends looking down
at you. Nothing is quite that bad now is it?

When you condition yourself to be capable
with nothing—not even the clothes you wear
on your body—and you enhance your ability
to draw on intrinsic survival knowledge,
emotional intelligence and muscle memory,
you can survive anywhere and without anything.
This is the essence of resilience. Anything
you happen to have with you when adversity
arrives is simply a bonus, expect to have
nothing and you can't be disappointed.

Pack list for a real survival kit:
Initiative
Improvisation
Creativity
Trial and error
Grit
Determination
Adaptability
Imagination
Visualisation
Humour

Always remain cognisant of the fact that:
"It is not the strongest of the species that survives,
nor the most intelligent that survives.
It is the one that is most adaptable to change."

—Charles Darwin

Section 2

Accepting the Now

Accepting the now is perhaps the hardest yet
fundamentally most vital aspect of survival.
You are where you are.
You are in the situation you are in.
You are there now.
Accept it and get on with it!

The Survival Oath

I accept full responsibility for the situation
I am in right at this moment.
I will not waste energy of any kind
attributing blame to others for this circumstance.
I am the master of my own destiny.
I will not be a victim in any way.
I will respond to the challenge the
universe has presented me with.
I will prevail.

Anger can be a very useful tool;
use it to focus your mind and body intently
on the tasks you must complete.
Never let it be converted to rage, however;
this path only leads to despair.
Control your anger!
Use it to your advantage!

When at an impasse, activate the mind of a child: play, sing, be curious, and allow yourself to *imagine*. Solutions will then appear!

When the veil of fear and panic closes around you,
just breathe;
in for four seconds,
hold for four seconds,
and out for four seconds.

Control and clear thought will return.
Practice this survival breathing as often as you can!

When you find yourself paralysed by fear and indecision, doing *anything* is generally a better option than doing *nothing* at all.

When the shock of a life-threatening situation
you face finally hits you,
STOPA:
Sit
Think
Observe
Plan
Act

Strive to be like water, and go with the flow.
Don't resist the situation you find yourself in.
To do so only wastes precious energy.

To survive or not to survive is a *choice*
you consciously make.
It's your decision which of those choices you go with.
It really is up to you!

No matter how bad things are right at this moment,
other human beings are facing and have faced
similar situations and have prevailed.
That is important knowledge because they were
not superhuman. They were people, just like you.
They came through, and so can you!

The Survival Tea Ceremony

When it is all too much and you feel completely
overwhelmed, sit down and make a cup of tea.
Make that tea with your full attention.
Make it very deliberately, and use the physical
actions of the process to expunge all thoughts of
your predicament. Allow your mind to be still.
Ask your heart rate to lower and your breathing
to slow. Drink the tea deliberately, focusing on its
flavour and warmth. Honour, the *Time*, *Energy*
and *Attention* (T.E.A) you have invested.
Only after the tea is finished should you pay
attention to thoughts regarding your situation.
At that moment, you will find that you are now in
a different emotional space, one with which you
can see with fresh eyes the problems you face.

"Tough times don't last; tough people do."
—Anonymous

When you get knocked clean off your feet,
stand back up, brush off the dust, and face up again.
Never stay down; keep getting straight back up.

The longer you spend denying
that something has happened to you,
the longer it will be until
you do something about it.

In the game of survival, you must focus your thoughts on what you need to do and only what you need to do. Your thoughts must be empowered by imagination and creativity such that you become adaptable. Adaptability is the key, non-linear and unconventional thought patterns are the path to an adaptable mindset. So focus your thoughts outside of the box.

If we allow ourselves to be a victim of our circumstances, we remain imprisoned. Emancipation from that prison is achieved by accepting total responsibility for our immediate present and our future. Ignore totally how, why and who led us to arrive at this place we now find ourselves. It is already no longer relevant to the present or the future. Leave it behind and walk forwards.

Whining and complaining thoughts and words weaken your resolve to prevail. Do not tolerate them in your own mind, do not speak them and quell them in others around you. If your words are not contributing to the solution then they are adding to the problem.

Section 3

Maintaining the Mindset
of a Survivor

Survival in any context is simply a very
personal combination of dynamic change
management and risk management.
To prevail in such circumstances,
we must—above all else—be adaptable.

What you *need* to survive and what you *want* to have at that moment are not necessarily related.

Be grateful for
every cup full of water,
every morsel of food,
every piece of firewood,
and every branch you build your shelter with.

Be truly grateful in your heart;
these simple things allow you to survive
yet another day. That is a true gift!

Prioritise, prioritise, prioritise!
Do only what is important to keep going. Keep
moving forward, keep making everything
you do count towards your survival.

You cannot waste
even a drop of sweat or a joule of energy.
You must make every effort you expend count
for something that will improve your lot.
Every cost to your body
must be rewarded with a positive gain.
Slow down, think, prioritise, and act wisely.

Consider that you are even here:
The odds have been totally against you
from the outset of conception, throughout
your existence in-utero, birth, and through
the journey of your entire life to this
point, yet here you are, reading this.
That qualifies you as a survivor right there!

So back yourself!
No matter what it is that you face, you
can get through it and keep surviving—
just as you have always done.

When you light fire in a survival situation,
you ignite a powerful feeling of *I can!*

In a survival situation the external environment impacts on your body directly and your internal thoughts, emotions and capabilities indirectly. Through the power of focus, we can empower our minds to shift the equation such that the internal dynamic we experience affects the external environment to our advantage.

Everything around you is a resource
willing you to use it
for something towards your survival.

In survival we can use our psychology to influence our physiology. By that I mean that we can use breath control to slow our heart rate and expand our awareness. Doing so eliminates fear and panic. We can employ strong personal body language to shift our emotions from that of a state of victimhood to action by simply standing up, standing tall and stepping forward. Bring it on!

Release the full power of your imagination
and creativity. Never has your life
depended on it as much as right now!

Every single item designed for one particular purpose can always be made to do at least three other things—*when you engage your imagination, release your creativity and tap into your unconventionality.*

A survival kit may come in a box, but to survive, it is imperative that you *think* outside of that box.

One way to sum up the attitude a survivor
must adopt is that they must:

"Improvise, adapt, and overcome."
—US Marine Corps mantra

Home is a place in your heart
that you can re-create anywhere.

The shelter you build is your castle;
it fortifies you in every way. It protects you from
the elements, but most importantly, it provides you
with a sense of place, a focal point, and a sanctuary
in a situation over which you have little control.

When your campfire burns brightly in the darkness,
the creatures lurking out there in the gloom
are driven further back. Always have a good
supply of firewood before darkness settles in.

When you lie down on the bare earth to sleep,
the Great Mother will embrace you, so do not
be afraid. Humans have always realised
that they belong to the Earth.
You are safe.
You are *home*.

When the going gets tough and the tough get going, *survivors* rest in the shade and conserve sweat and calories.

Real survival is simple.
Pick up the left foot, and place it in front
of the right foot. Pick up the right foot,
and place it in front of the left foot.

Now just keep doing that.
Left, right, left, right.

Before you do anything:

"Observe, orientate, decide, act!"

—Colonel John Boyd

Keep your hands busy and your mind quiet. When time drags and you think too much you start believing things that are simply not real. Your mind conspires to convince you that you need to do more than you are doing. You start putting deadlines on things where there is no necessity to do so. You start making decisions that don't need to be made. You start wasting energy and you start dying.
Busy hands; quiet mind!

In a survival situation,
you are going to have low moments.

That's just the way it is; accept it. Tell yourself not to
react to those low-vibrational thoughts; let them pass.
While in their tenacious grip, don't do too much.
Definitely don't make any major decisions.
The low feelings and sense of despair will pass.

Talk all you like, but do more.

Hang on for another minute, another hour, another day, another week. That's your only task. Hang on!

Survivors are rarely the loudest, most vocal, or most popular individuals in a group. They are the individuals who simply begin doing what needs to be done.

In a survival situation, everyone involved has a stake in the outcome, so everyone must have a voice in the decisions that are made. Regardless of this process however, decisions must still be made. You can't just talk about it forever. At some point after everyone has had their say you have to convert words to action.

The quietest, youngest, most inexperienced and unlikely person in a group can come up with the most practical solution to the most complex of problems. If you are the leader, be sure to listen to everyone.

"No matter how bad you feel, how much you wish to wallow in your own misery, when things need to be done, you just need to get up and do them!"
—Rebel H.

Live by your wits and intelligence,
and trust your intuition.

Boredom while waiting to be returned to civilisation can be a significant test. Each day plan and accomplish some small task, something you can do easily without great effort. Something that will improve your lot in some small way. Make a tool, improve your shelter, go fishing, build a fishing net, it doesn't matter really what it is. Boredom can actually kill you, keep it at bay and let small successes add up to survival.

Pain is a good thing; it means you are
still *alive!* Use it as your compass.

Quitting is always a choice you will regret later.
Focus your attention on never entertaining or
tolerating any thoughts of giving up, ever.

Your life matters; it matters to you, and it matters to the people who love and care for you. You have a duty above all else to make it back to them in one piece. Commit to that duty, get up and keep going!

Anchor your emotions strongly to the desire to return to your loved ones. To hold them and cry with them, to see their smiles and look into their eyes one more time. With such a powerful anchor, you will succeed!

When your number is up and it is finally time for you to leave this world, so be it; accept it with grace. However, until that choice is made for you, you just keep going, keep surviving, and keep living.

If you work aggressively against nature, fighting it and viewing it as the enemy, you will waste a lot of energy, and survival will be hard. Learn to work smoothly with the natural rhythms, ebbs, and flows of nature around you. You will instantly discover that things get easier.

In a group of survivors you have to hand a library
of many books, all with knowledge, wisdom,
and experience to draw on to help you overcome
the obstacles you face. Alone you have just one
shelf of books to seek answers within. There
is consequently real power in the group.

Keep it simple stupid (KISS); the simpler anything is, the fewer things can go wrong with it, and the easier it is to do when you are exhausted.

When you look deeply into the warming
flames of your campfire, you may discover that
you can go anywhere in your mind. You can
achieve anything with the many gifts you have
been blessed with, and you will then know
that you will get through whatever is next.

Attacking nature, cutting and hacking your way through the bush, burns up precious energy and water. Slow down, breathe deep, look around; there is usually an easier path close by.

Think laterally, and condition yourself to see what others cannot when they are blinded by habit or their ability to think clearly is obscured by fear and panic. This provides you with an enormous advantage, one that may just keep you alive.

"When you have gone so far that you cannot go one more step then you have gone just half the distance that you are capable of."
—Greenland proverb

Survival leaders are those individuals who consistently
make the soundest decisions and act on them.
Why? Because people prefer to move away from
pain and discomfort and towards ease and comfort.
Survival leaders make fewer bad choices and the
people suffer fewer negative consequences.

Humans are animals, too, so they will always seek to move away from pain and discomfort towards ease and comfort. Understand this!

Focus totally on all that you love—your family, your friends, your faith, your life. Concentrate your total attention on your memory of them. Cry, let the heart yearn—use this emotion to drive you onwards.

If it is hot, do not dwell on that fact as you will only feel more heat. If you are cold, do not focus on that, or the cold will become intolerable. If your hunger threatens to unravel you, put it aside in your mind. If your thirst is unquenchable, do not pay attention to it. You have tasks to complete and a job to do. Direct all of your attention and energy to this work alone.

To survive is a matter of choice. You can choose to be a victim, or you can choose to be a responder and help yourself. Choose now!

"Never, never, never give up!"
—Winston Churchill

Everyone in your survival group is facing an internal battle of self-control, just trying desperately to keep it together ... just as you are. They are scared out of their minds. Be gentle with each other.

When calamity is upon us and those around us lose all hope, warriors and survivors lead the way back to it.

"If you're going through hell, keep on going."
—Rodney Atkins (American Country Music Artist)

Dare to be unconventional. Being unconventional means you can be more adaptable. Survival is totally about your ability to adapt rapidly. Dare to walk a different path, dare to win.

Trust your gut. If something doesn't feel right, it probably isn't right. Act on that.

Don't just go along with everyone else. Listen to your intuition, and be prepared to lead or make a different decision from the others. Group thinking can often be wrong thinking.

You can ask, "Why me?" Or you can say, "Thank you for giving me this amazing adventure!" It is simply a matter of perspective.

The individual who knows the power of
their own mind survives longest.

Every time you go away from those you love, vow that
no matter what, you will come back. When survival
becomes your reality, every night before you close
your eyes to sleep, remind yourself of that promise.
You will make it back to them; you will come back!

"F.E.A.R is simply an acronym for False
Expectations Appearing Real."
—Anonymous

Never underestimate the power of humour even in the blackest of moments. Laugh whenever you can, at whatever you can. Laugh at each other, laugh at yourself, laugh at the situation. Laugh out loud and giggle until your sides hurt.

The way you perceive the world around you is
dependent on what filters you have enabled.
You have the power to adjust those filters
to reduce your level of perceived fear.

I—AM a survivor!

About the Author

Rich Hungerford founded the Bush Lore Australia Survival school in 2010. A former Australian Special Air Service (SAS) soldier and instructor, Rich now teaches survival, tracking, and bushcraft at his Bush Lore School. Through Bush Lore, Rich continues to explore his instinctive passion for the natural world in order to pass his extensive experience on to others. He has the gift of being able to successfully blend both his real world military experience and naturalist perspectives of survival and bushcraft in a way that offers students access to a unique depth of knowledge in bushcraft, tracking, and survival skills. Rich teaches what works and only what works, he refuses to pass on flawed or unproven knowledge, skills and concepts. Consequently, his personal journey with the fascinating subject of survival and bushcraft have seen him immerse himself deeply in research, practice and observation. It is a journey that Rich himself has stated, has no end. *The more you know the more you realise how much you have yet to learn.*

Much of what Rich has learned has been through actual immersion in the wilderness, usually alone and in remote locations for long periods of time. It is in these places that one has to draw fully on what is within. There is no immediate source of assistance, everything must be necessarily tackled head on with what is at hand. It is during these situations that the white noise of fear and anxiety is loudest in your head. *You have to shut that down and just get on with things.* It consequently fosters an attitude of imagination, unconventionality, creativity, doggedness, determination and absolute self-reliance.

Rich has always been particularly interested in this psychology of survival, the intriguing facets of the human mind that largely determine who survives and who doesn't when faced with a life-threatening situation. This mindset has an impact on the individual survivor regardless of how the situation develops. Accordingly, Rich trains students to deal with survival anywhere, anytime, and in any circumstance. In wilderness or urban spaces, alone or as a group, in short-term or long-term situations. *To be a survivor one has to be comfortable in chaos.* The linchpin behind his approach is to develop in his students the concept of *how to think to survive*. How to wire thoughts and emotions together such that they work towards solutions rather than a growing sense of hopelessness.

After experiencing various military deployments to conflict zones and having had the opportunity to study first hand the survival mindset of many in the midst of real-time adverse situations, an entire philosophy of survival has evolved in Rich's understanding and teaching of the subject. Other philosophical and martial influences in his life have left this modern warrior with a drive and passion to empower individuals, their families, and communities to be resilient in the face of disaster no matter what form it takes. *To be ready for what's next, whatever it is.*

Rich successfully blends emotional intelligence, leadership, survival psychology, and traditional survival and bushcraft skills to deliver a complete approach to survival in all its forms. *It is a warrior's duty to survive; to continue to be of use, and to protect his or her family, friends and community.* To be a true warrior, one must by definition be spiritual for spirituality is ultimately a warrior's path. It is a path towards the development of a higher self, it is a path of service to others. It is a path that polishes the mirror of the soul. It is a path Rich has always followed, and the one he continues to walk. It is the path of the survivor.